From

MW01045261

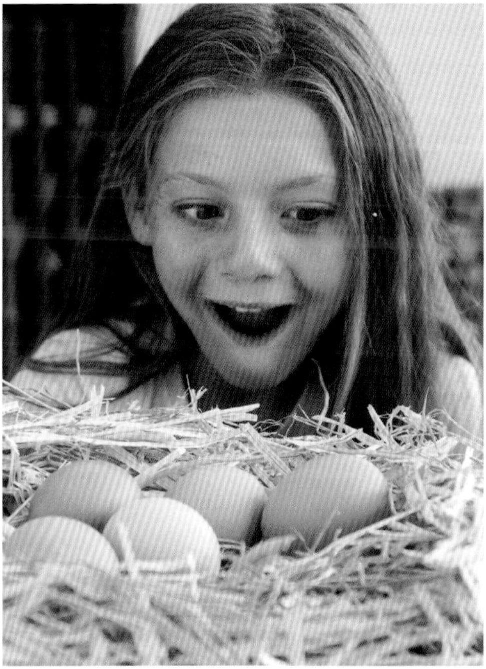

written by Pam Holden

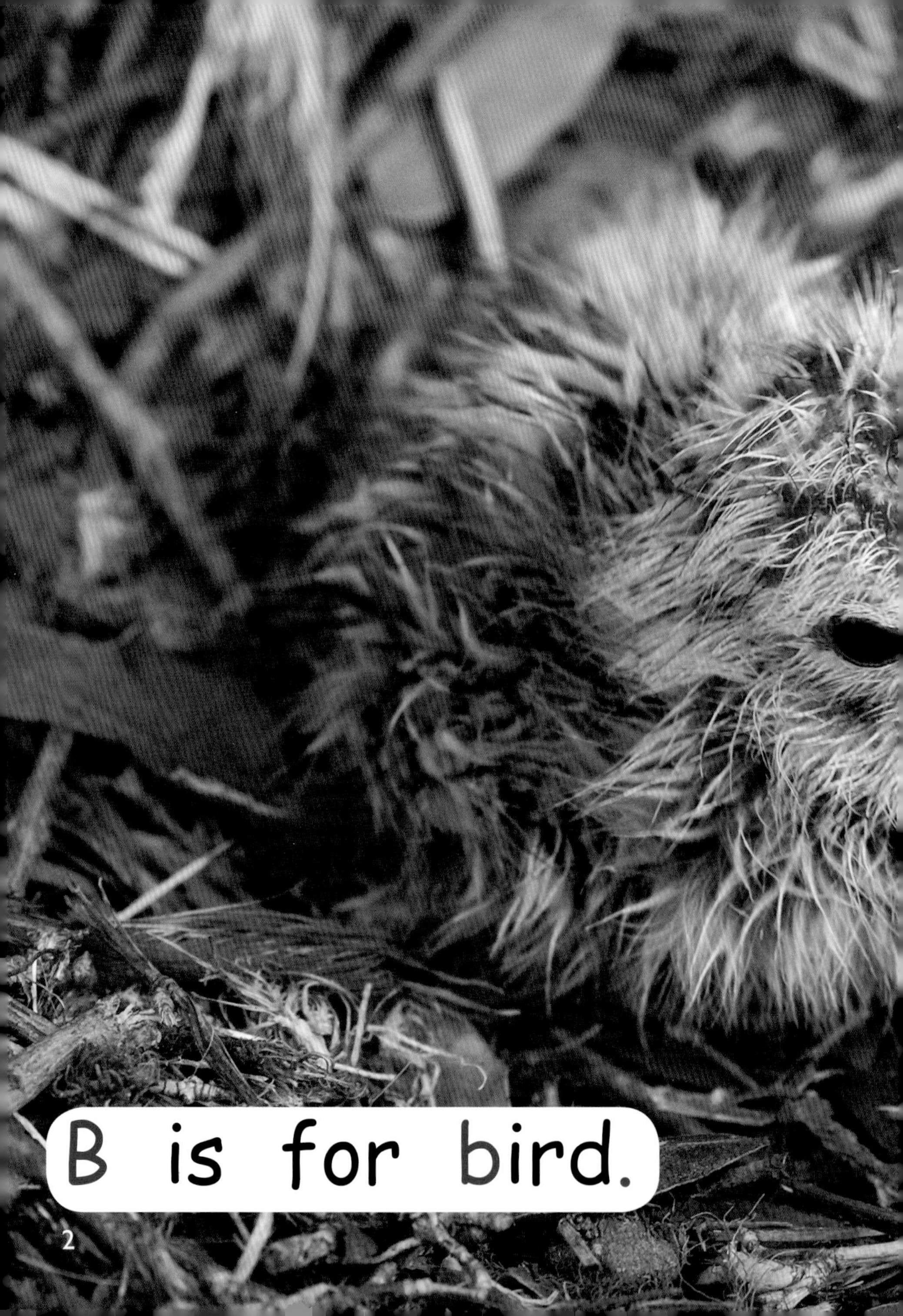

B is for bird.

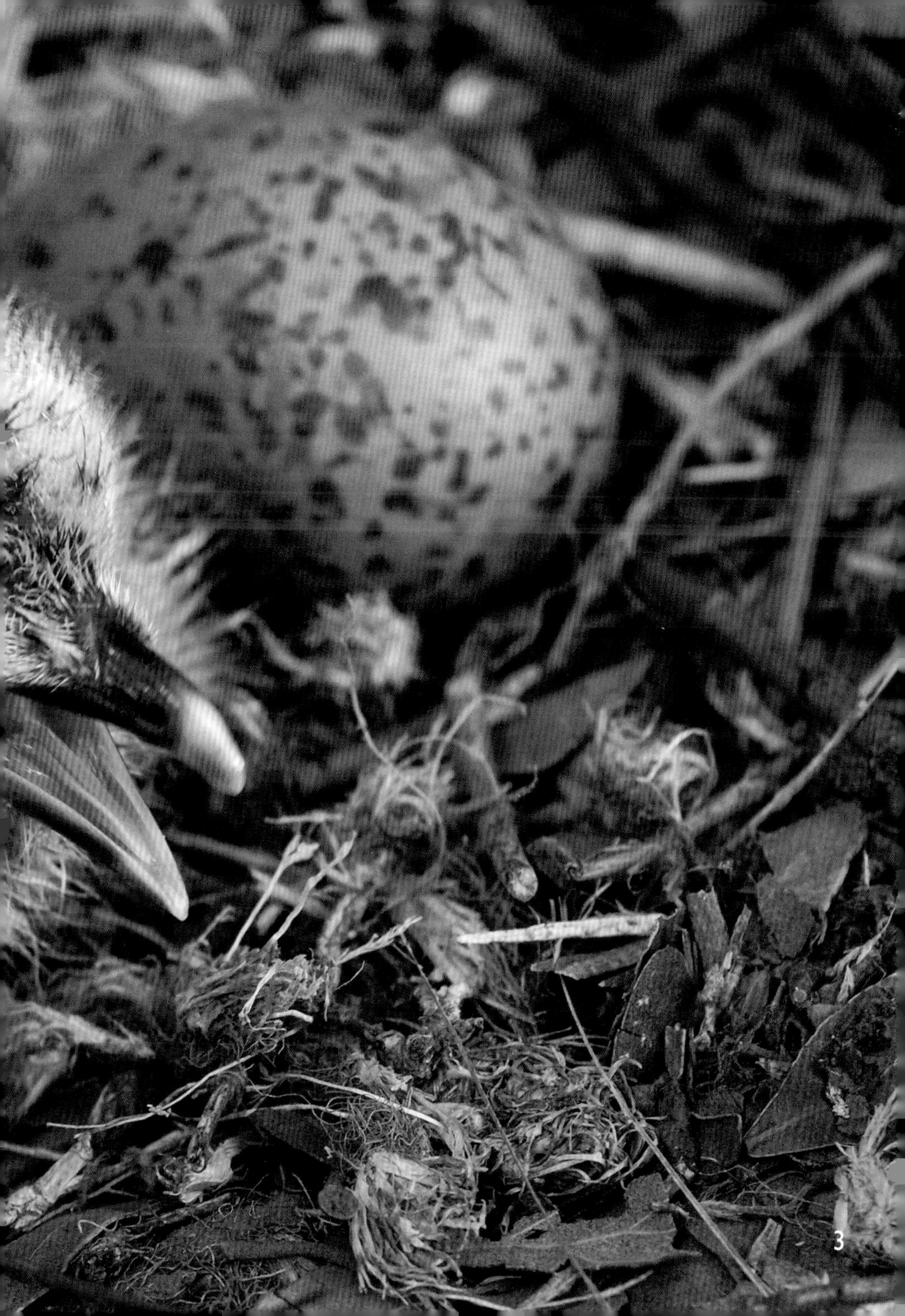

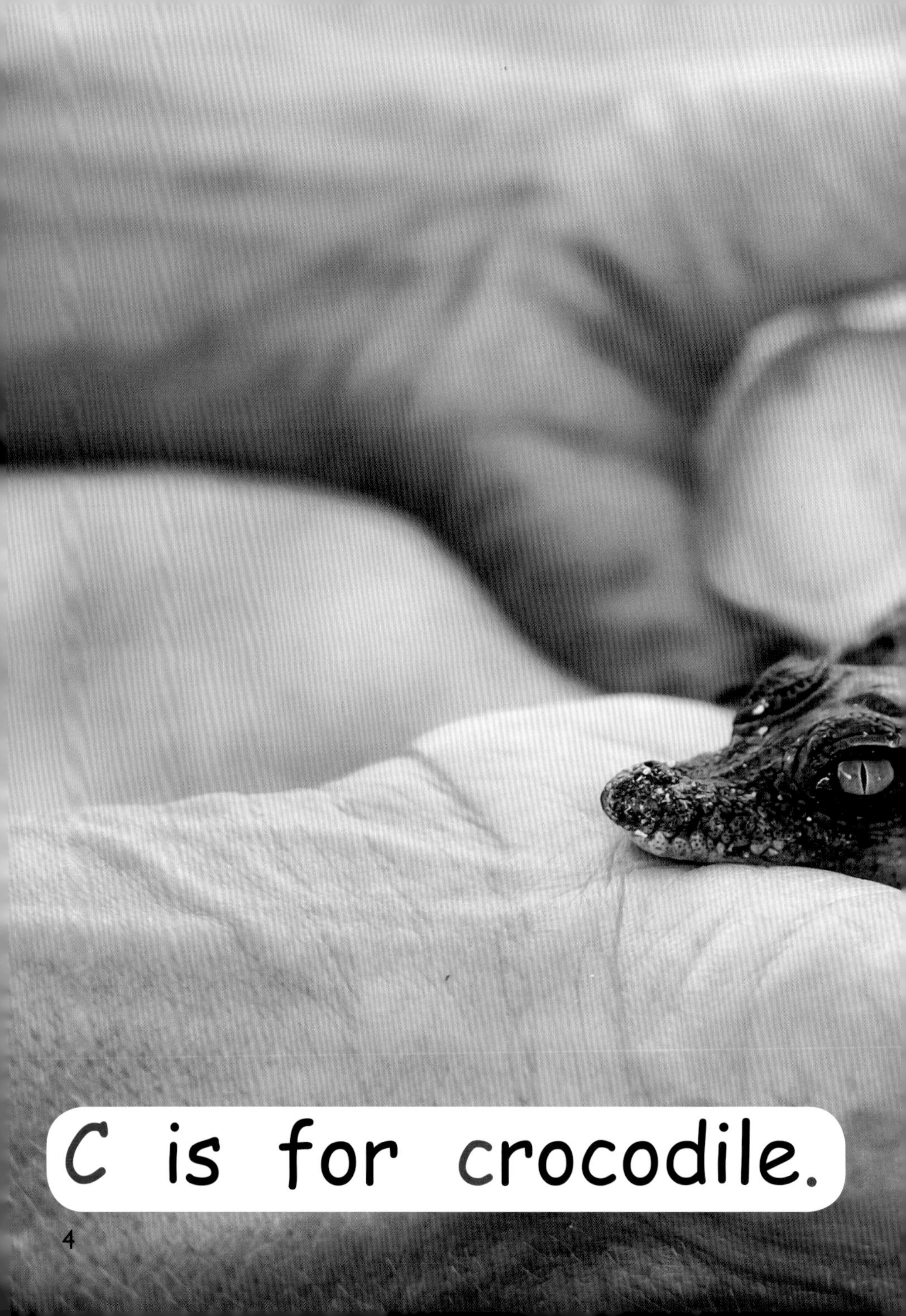

C is for crocodile.

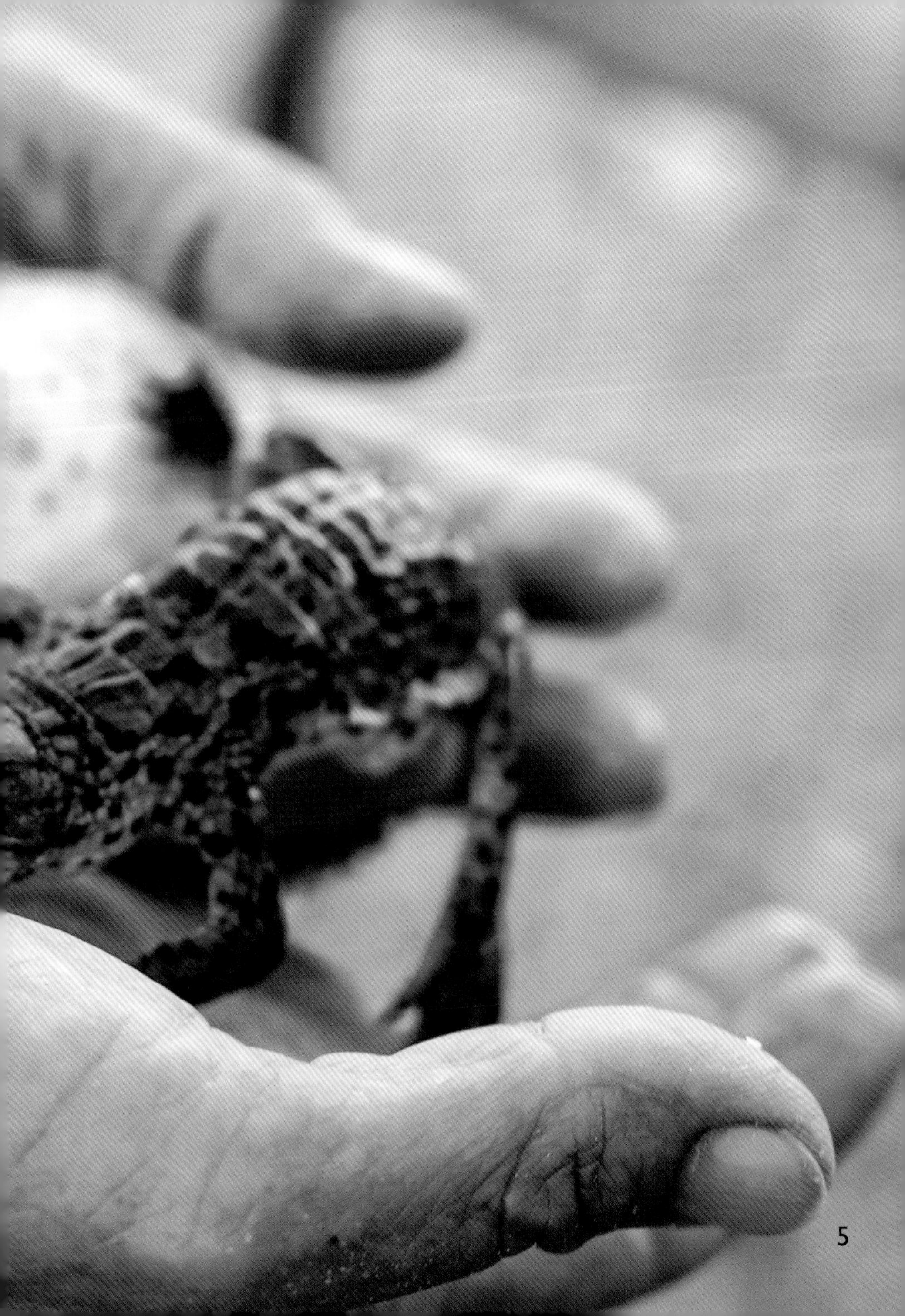

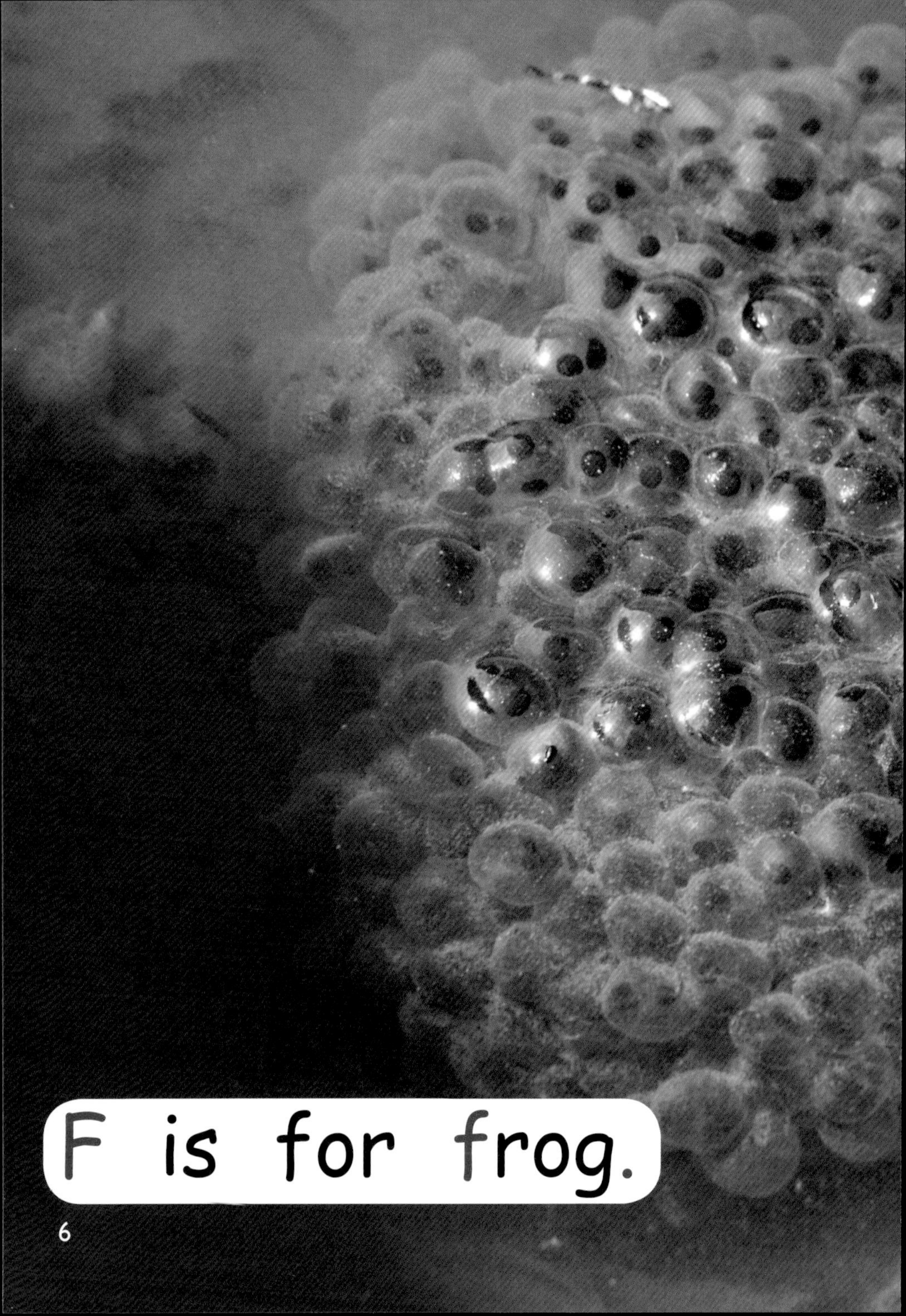

F is for frog.

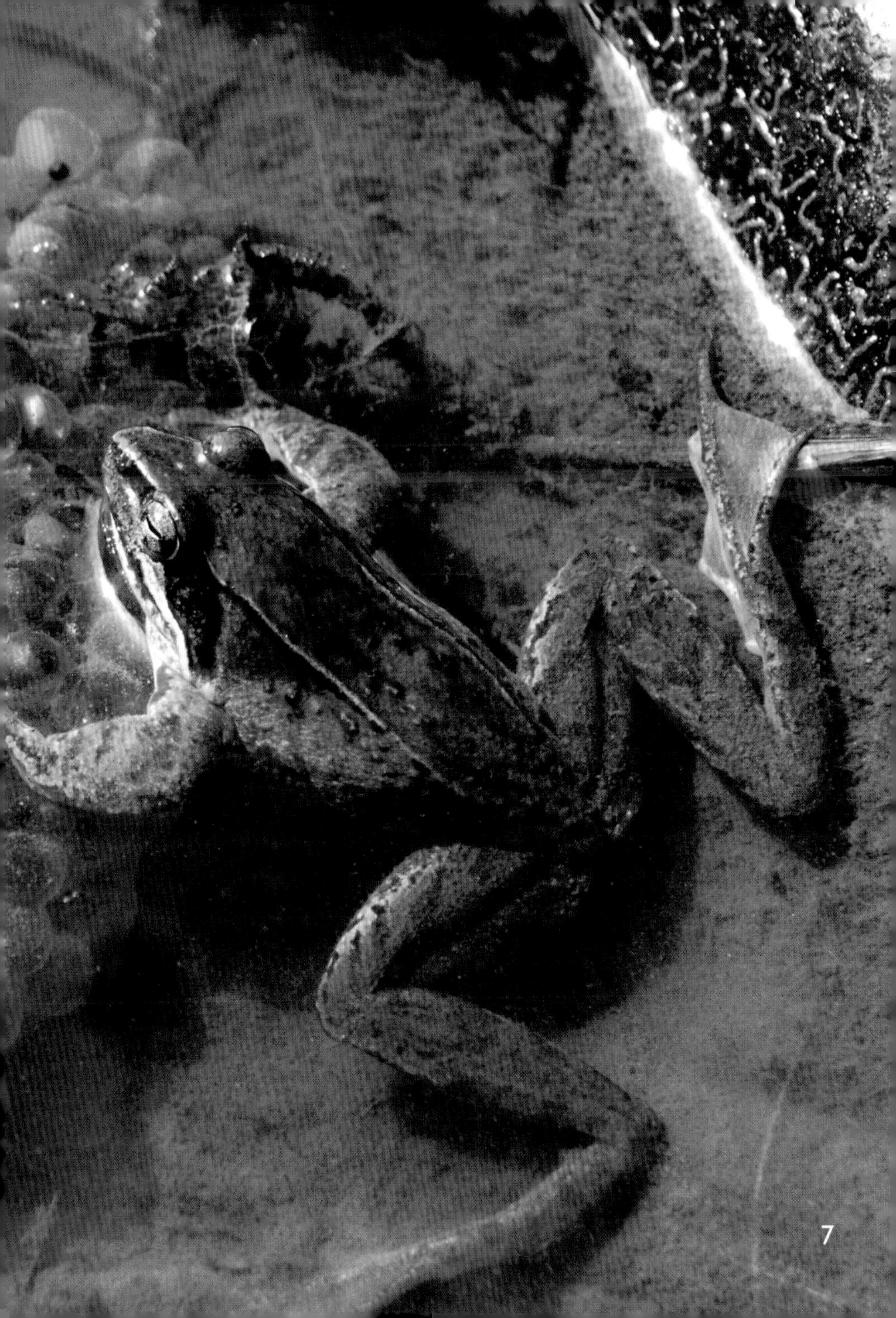

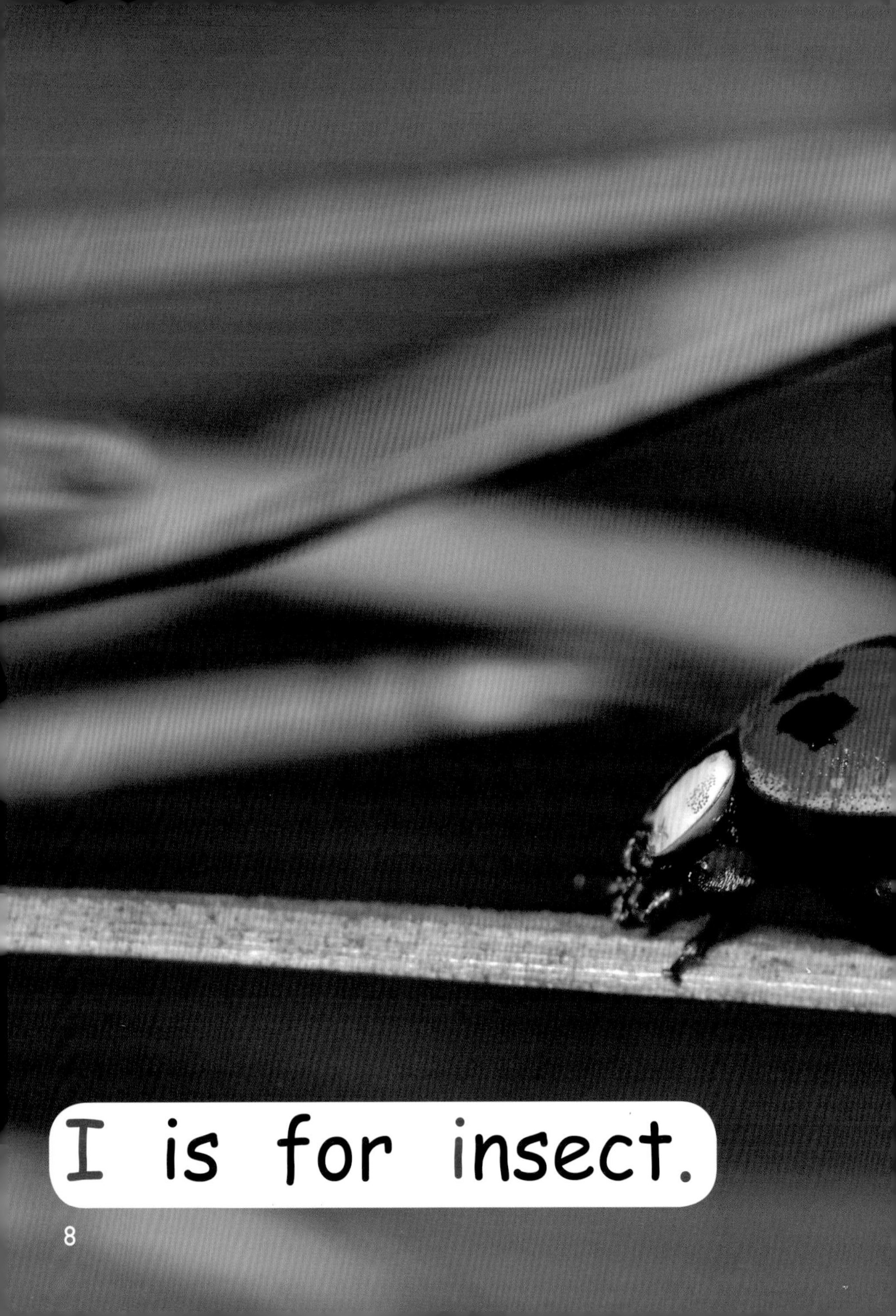

I is for insect.

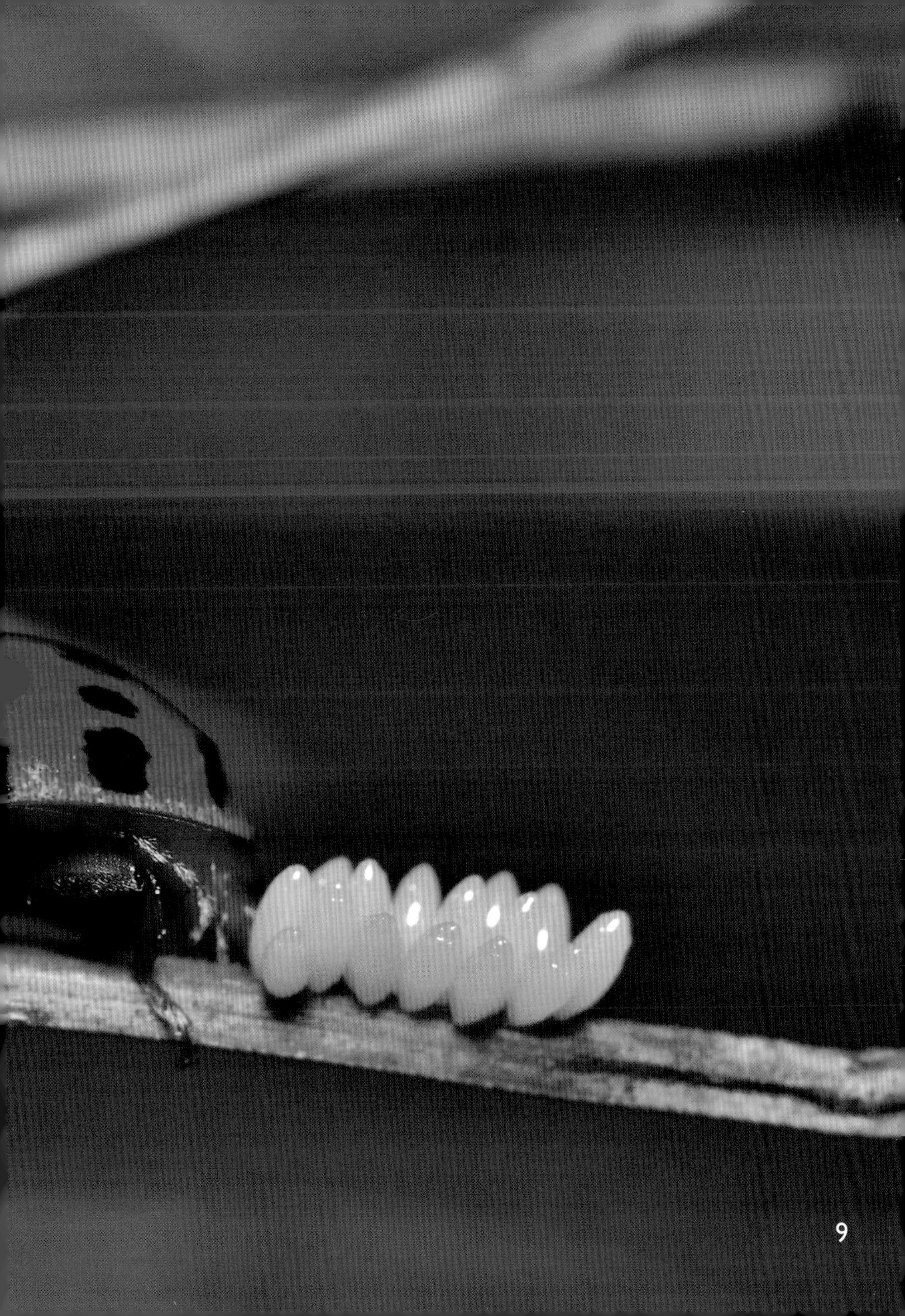

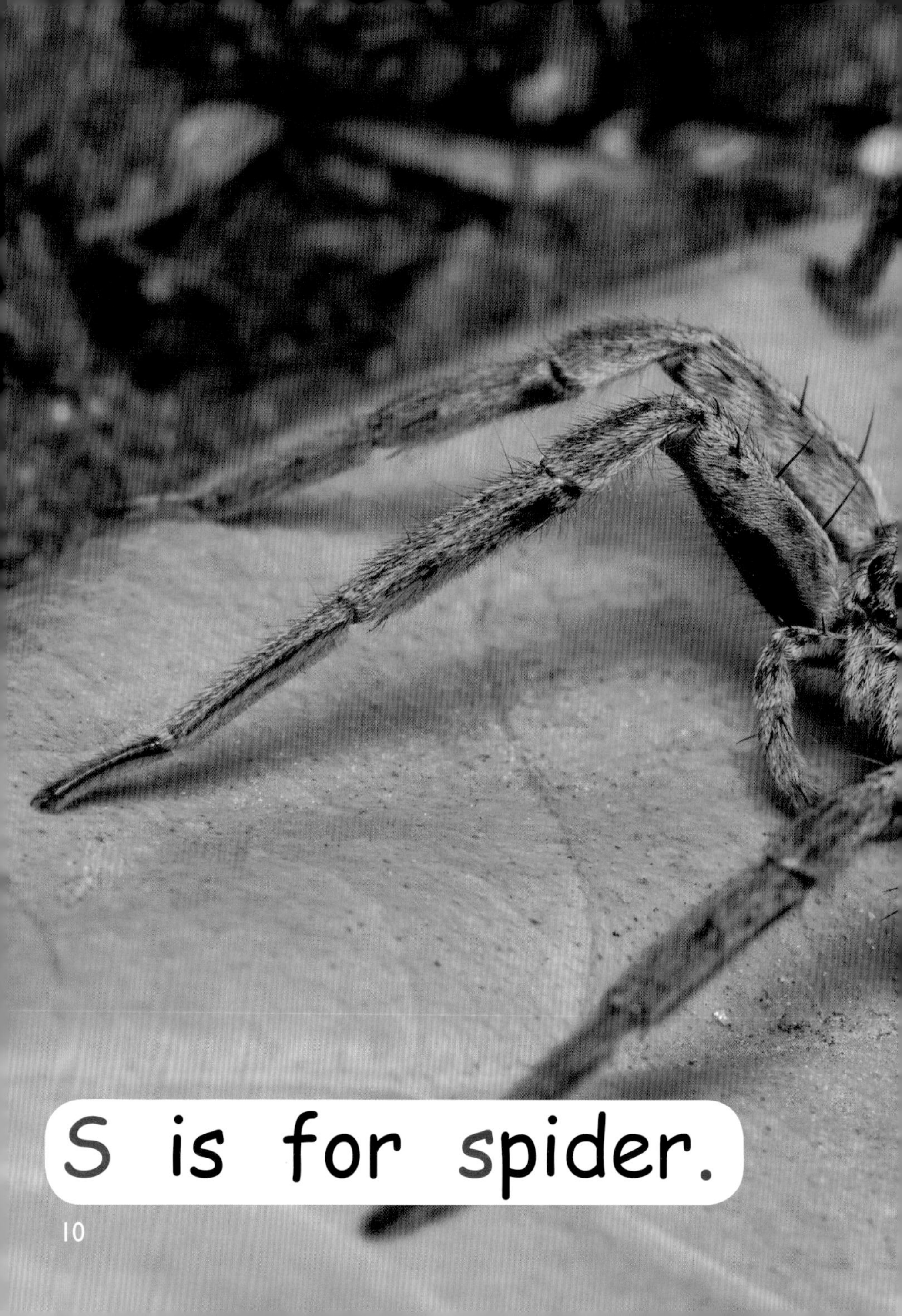

S is for spider.

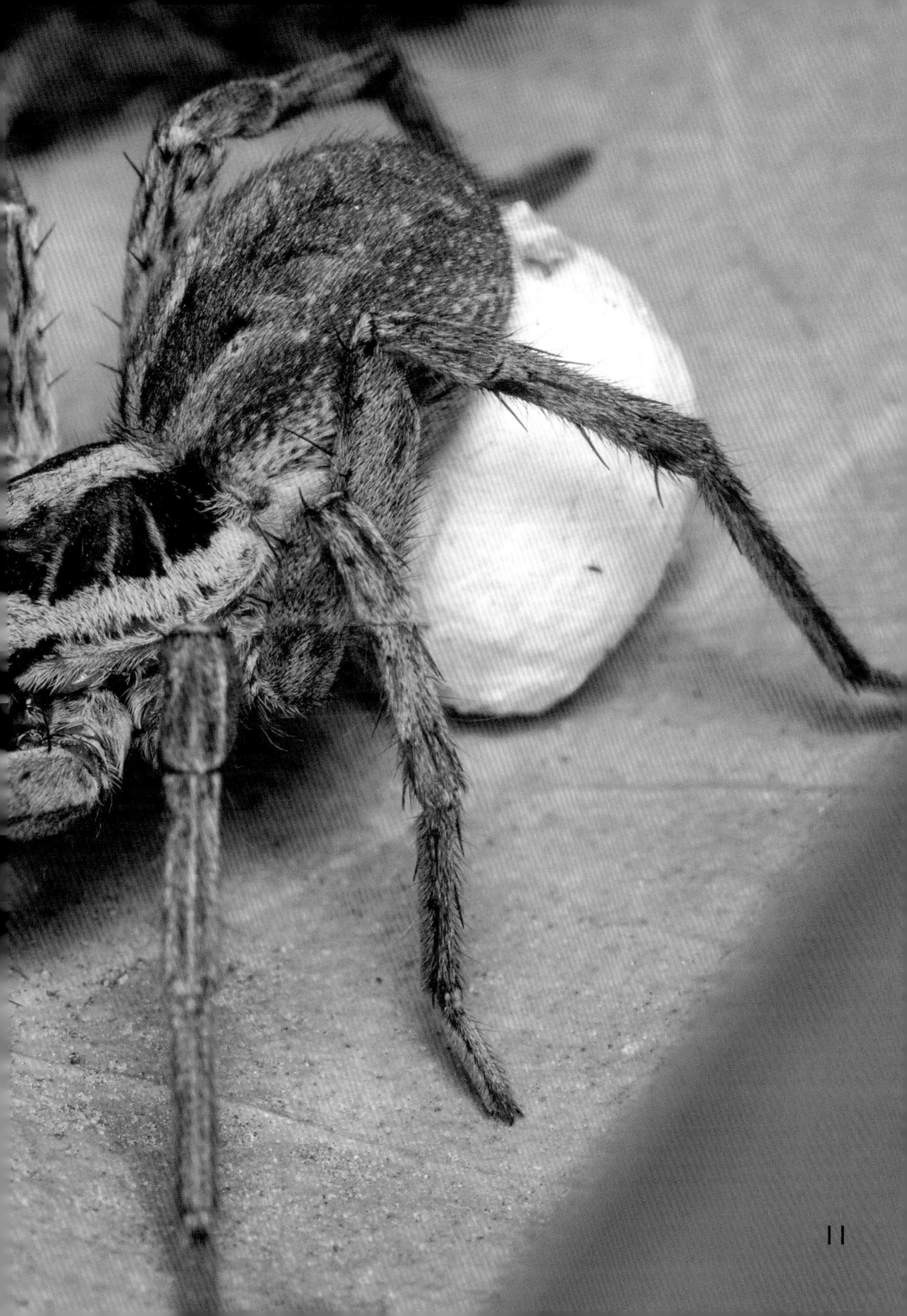

T is for turtle.

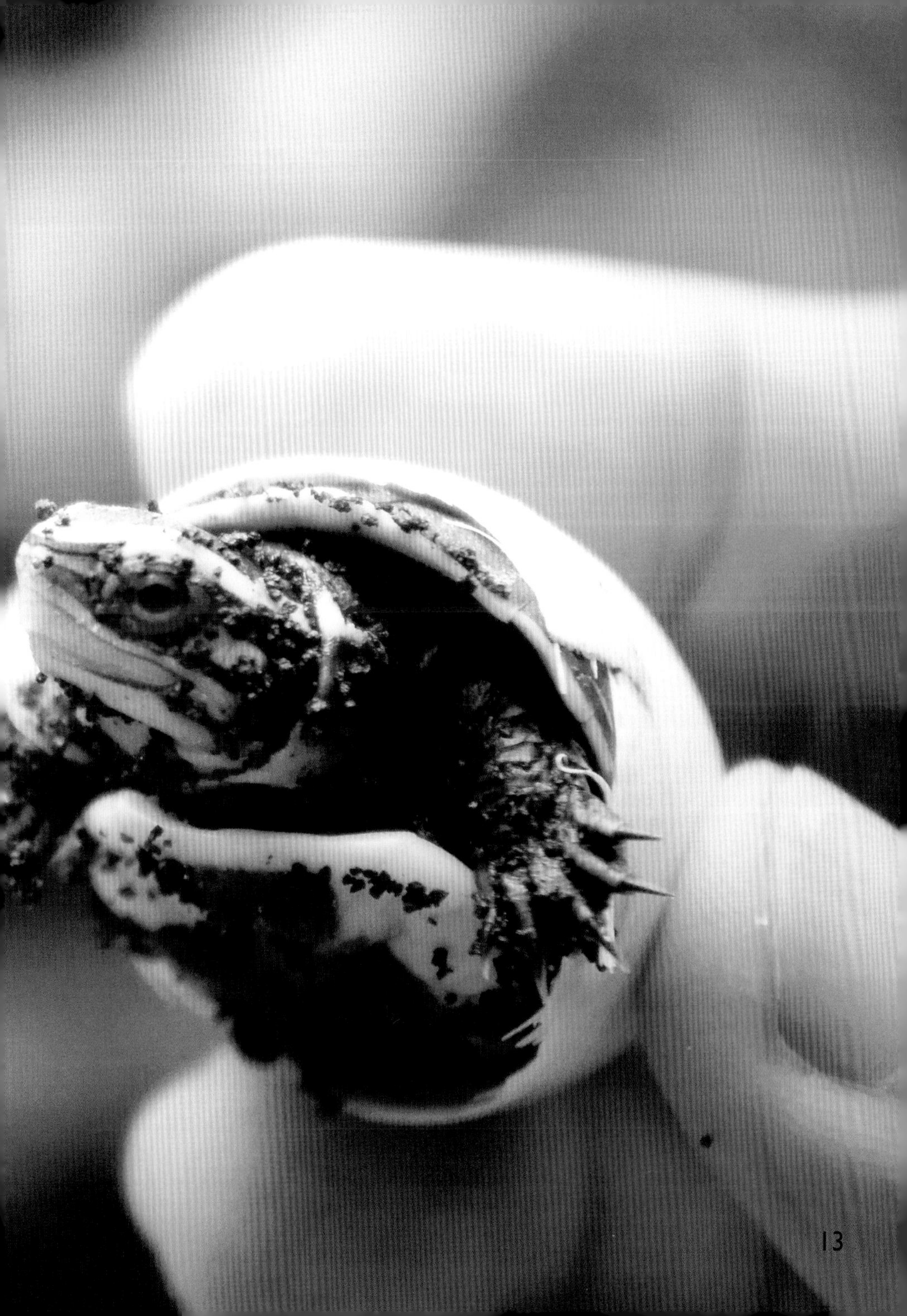

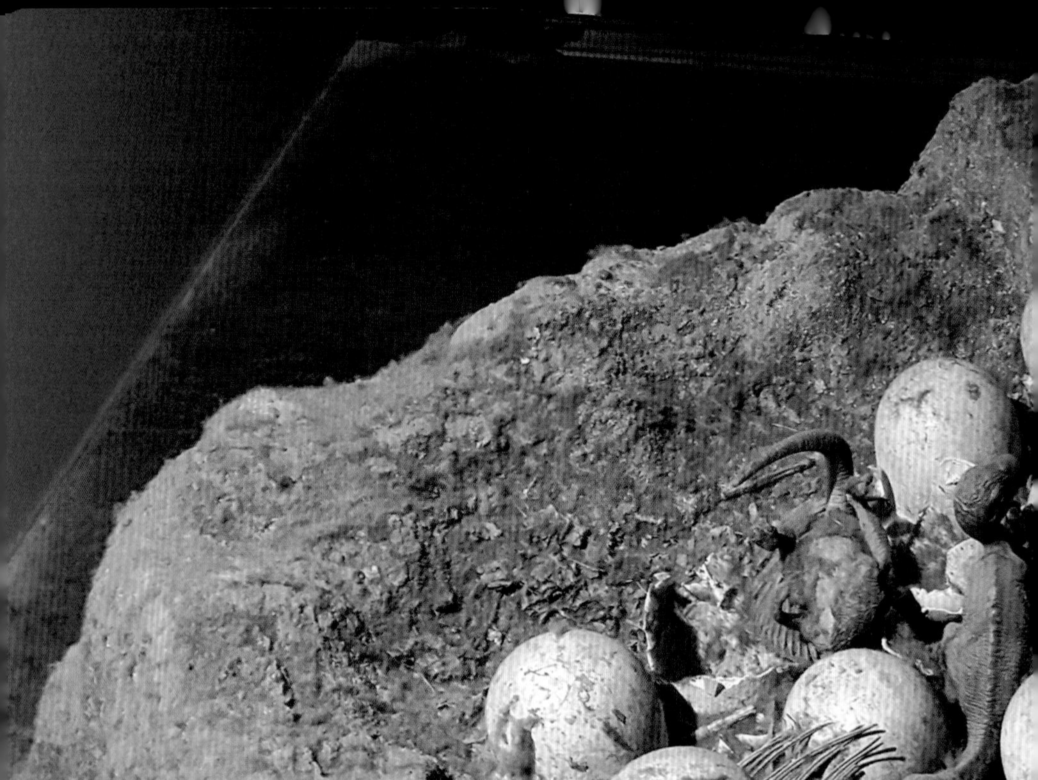

D is for dinosaurs.

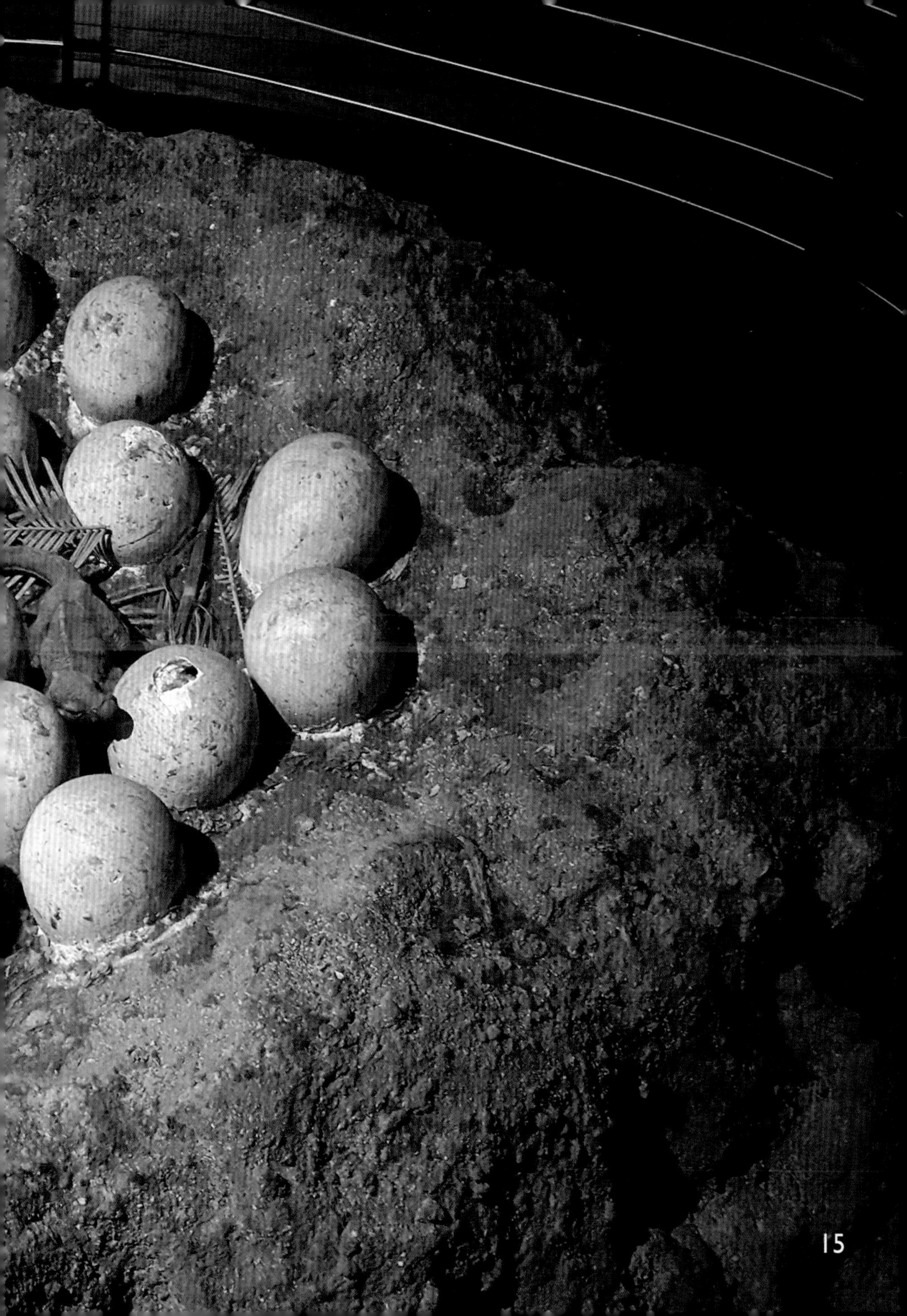

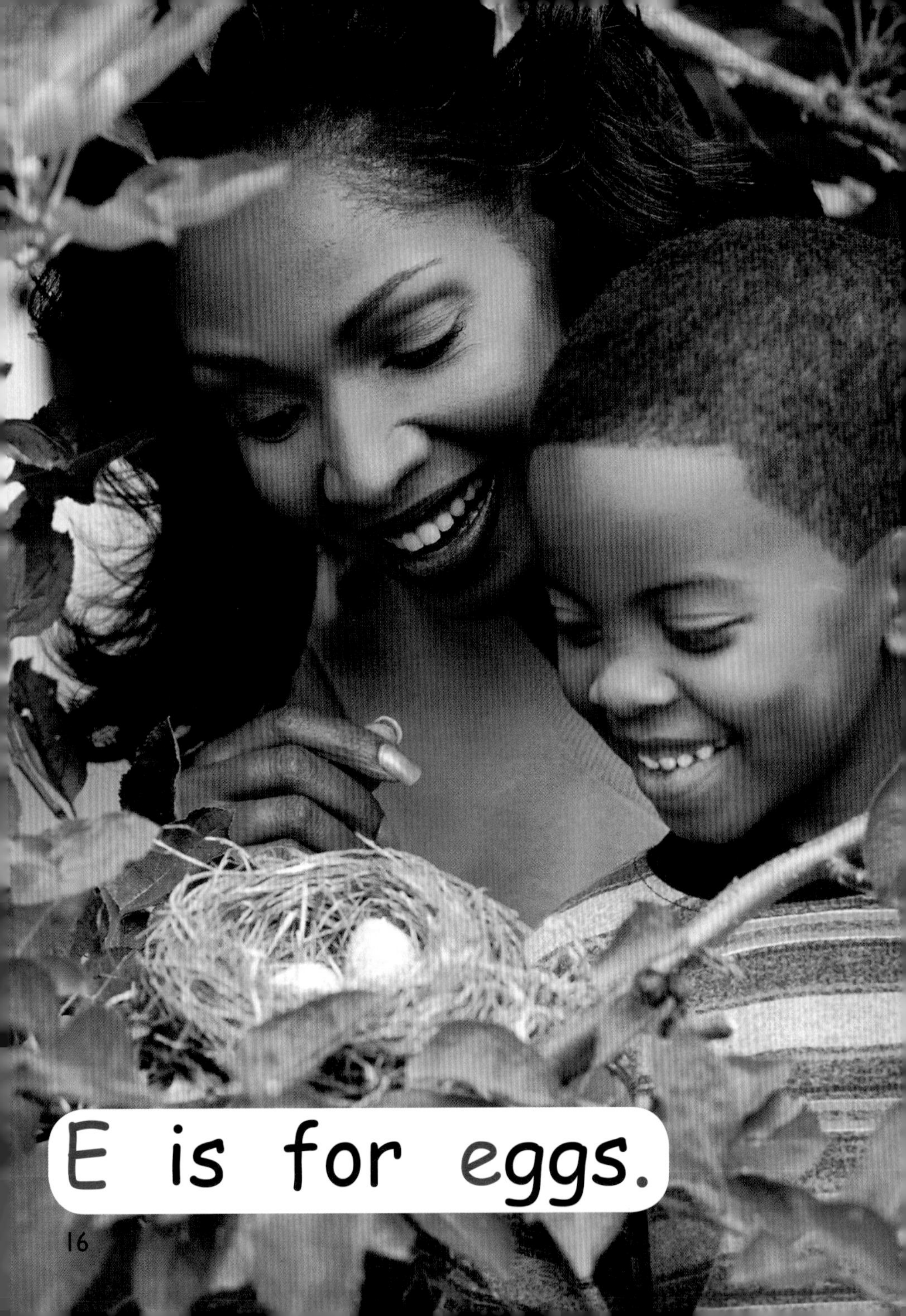

E is for eggs.